MISSION CONTROL

THE PARKER SOLAR PROBE

JENNIFER LOMBARDO

PowerKiDS press

Published in 2025 by The Rosen Publishing Group, Inc.
2544 Clinton Street, Buffalo, NY 14224

First Edition

Editor: Jennifer Lombardo
Book Design: Rachel Rising

Photo Credits: Cover Jbruiz/Shutterstock.com; cover, p. 1, 3–32 KK.KICKIN/Shutterstock.com; p. 4 https://en.m.wikipedia.org/wiki/File:Parker_Solar_Probe_insignia.png; pp. 5, 7 NASA/Goddard/SDO; p. 8 Suliman Razvan/Shutterstock.com; p. 9 Juliasuena/Shutterstock.com; p. 10 Elena11/Shutterstock.com; p. 11 (probe) https://en.m.wikipedia.org/wiki/File:Parker_Solar_Probe_spacecraft_model.png; p. 11 (background) wing-wing/Shutterstock.com; p. 12 buradaki/Shutterstock.com; p. 15 D1min/Shutterstock.com;p. 16 https://en.m.wikipedia.org/wiki/File:Parker_Solar_Probe.jpg; p. 17 NASA/Johns Hopkins APL/Ed Whitman; p. 19 KatarzynaWozniak/Shutterstock.com; p. 20 https://en.m.wikipedia.org/wiki/File:Solar_eclipse_1806Jun16-Corona-Ferrer.png; p. 21 frederic bouvier/Shutterstock.com; p. 22 Naeblys/Shutterstock.com; p. 23 NASA's Goddard Space Flight Center/Lisa Poje/Genna Duberstein; pp. 24, 28 muratart/Shutterstock.com; p. 25 https://en.m.wikipedia.org/wiki/File:YoungAlfven.jpg; p. 26 NicoElNino/Shutterstock.com; p. 27 Mikael Damkier/Shutterstock.com; p. 29 Slometo/Shuttcrstock.com.

Library of Congress Cataloging-in-Publication Data
Names: Lombardo, Jennifer.
Title: The Parker Solar Probe / Jennifer Lombardo.
Description: Buffalo, NY : PowerKids Press, 2025. | Series: Mission control | Includes glossary and index.
Identifiers: ISBN 9781499449877 (pbk.) | ISBN 9781499449884 (library bound) | ISBN 9781499449891 (ebook)
Subjects: LCSH: Parker Solar Probe (Spacecraft)--Juvenile literature. | Sun--Juvenile literature. | Sun--Corona--Juvenile literature.
Classification: LCC QB521.5 L66 2025 | DDC 629.43'57--dc23

Manufactured in the United States of America

CPSIA Compliance Information: Batch #CWPK25. For further information contact Rosen Publishing at 1-800-237-9932.

CONTENTS

OUR CLOSEST STAR

Astronomers have been studying stars for thousands of years. As technology has advanced, they have been able to learn things such as how stars are born, what they are made of, and how hot they are. However, there are some things they can only learn by getting up close.

Studying our sun in depth will answer many questions astronomers still have. Not only will it tell us more about stars in general, it will help us understand the sun better. The sun is necessary for life on Earth, but it can also cause problems. For example, its ultraviolet (UV) **radiation** can cause skin **cancer**, and solar flares can make cell phones and other technology malfunction, or not work properly. Knowing more about the positives and negatives of the sun can be very helpful.

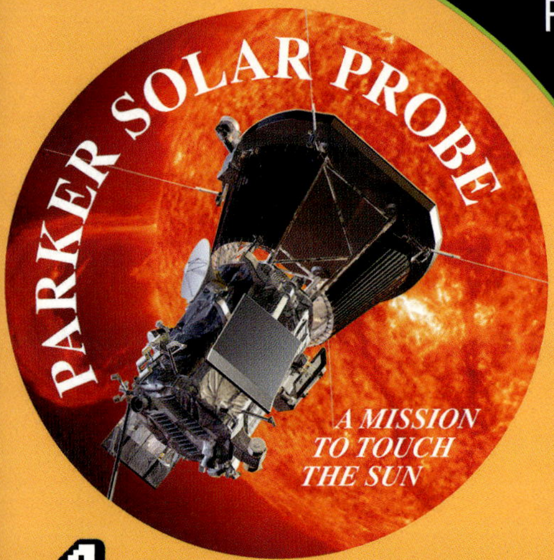

SOLAR FLARES

A solar flare is an explosion on the sun. The explosion sends charged particles flying at high speeds, allowing them to reach farther into space than normal. Some are almost too weak to be noticed. However, the stronger solar flares can reach as far as our planet. Strong solar flares can damage satellites and even some ground-based power grids, causing cell phone and power outages.

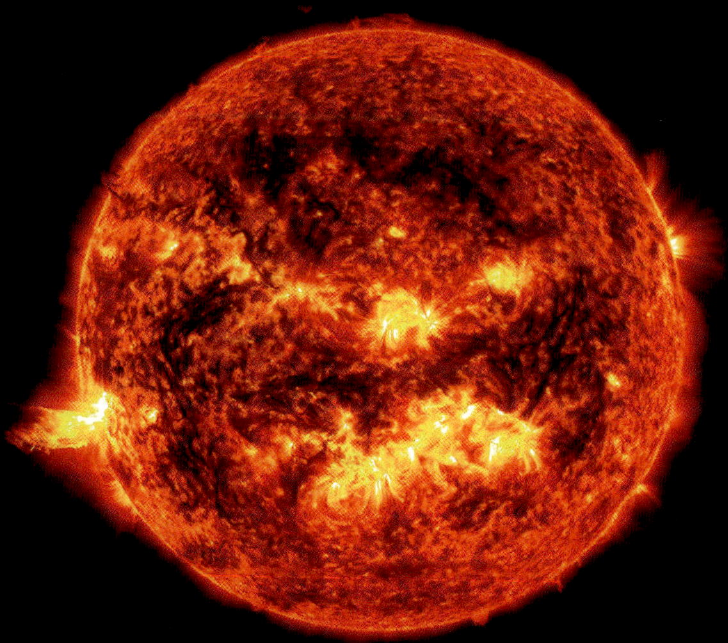

This picture of the sun was taken by NASA scientists using special cameras. The sun's light is so intense that it can permanently damage a regular camera.

STUDYING THE SUN

Because the sun is so hot and emits so much radiation, it is not safe for any person to get close to it. To study the sun in detail, astronomers had to build a probe that could withstand intense heat. It also needed instruments that could measure various aspects, or parts, of the sun. Astronomers were looking for answers to several questions, including:

- Why is the sun's **corona** much hotter than its surface?
- Where do high-energy solar particles come from?
- How does solar wind accelerate, or speed up, in space?

To get data that could help them answer these questions, astronomers focused on studying magnetic fields, plasma, and high-energy particles. They also added an instrument that could image, or take pictures of, the solar wind.

NASA KNOWLEDGE

A probe is an unmanned spacecraft loaded with instruments, or tools, to measure and record data in space.

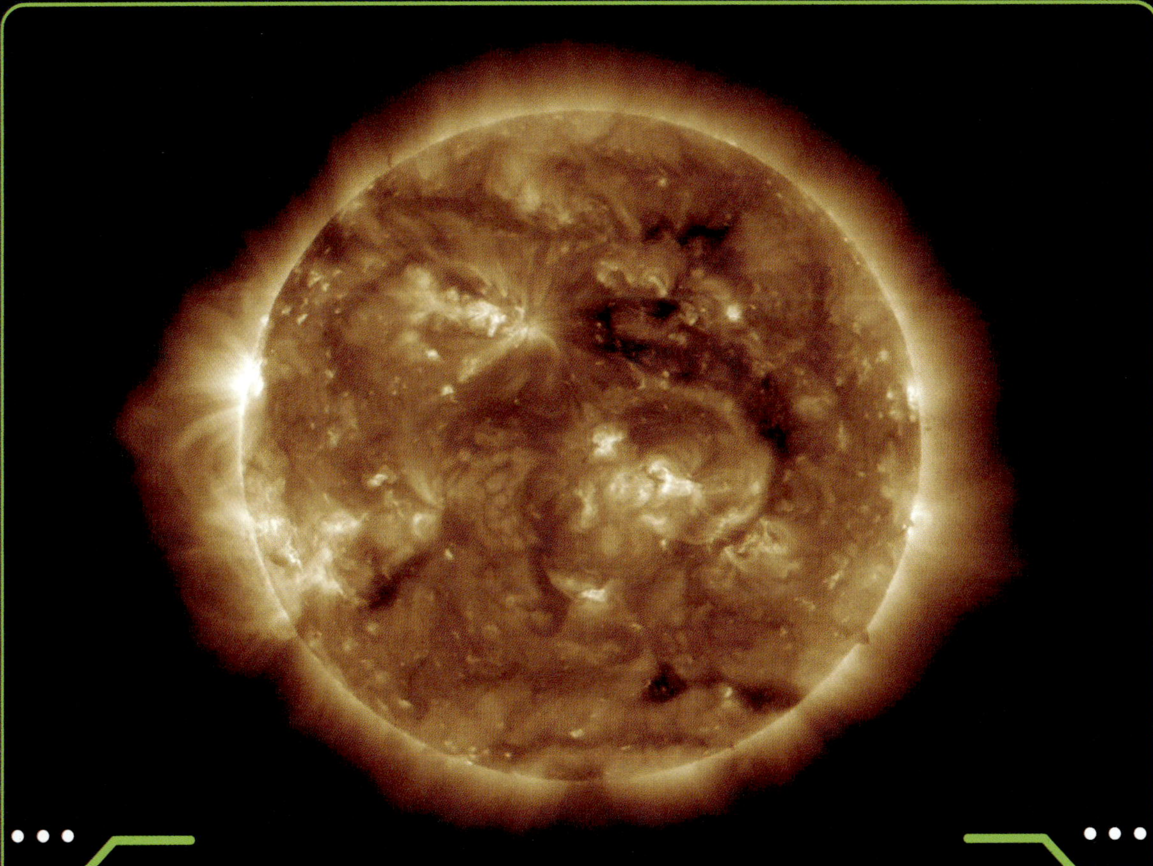

The sun's corona can be more than 2 million degrees Fahrenheit (1.1 million degrees Celsius). Its surface is about 10,000 degrees F (5,538 degrees C).

PARKER'S TOOLS

To answer their questions about the sun, the team creating the probe had to make several **specialized** instruments. To measure the solar wind, they made a tool called the Solar Wind Electrons Alphas and Protons Investigation (SWEAP). This tool counts the particles in solar wind.

To image the solar wind, they included a telescope called the Wide-field Imager for Solar Probe Plus (WISPR). This telescope creates 3D pictures of the corona and inner **heliosphere** so scientists can see the solar wind and try to figure out which part of the sun it comes from. To do this, WISPR uses heat shields to block most of the sun's light so it doesn't overpower the fainter light of the corona.

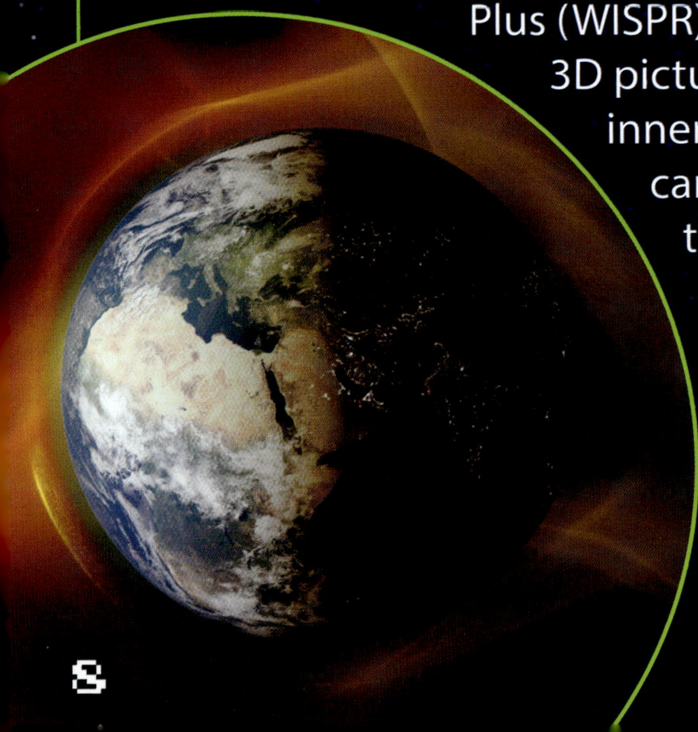

EUGENE PARKER

Because so much of the probe's work will be with solar wind, it was named after the man who came up with that term. In the 1950s, Eugene Newman Parker proposed several theories, or ideas, about how stars give off energy. These theories were later confirmed with advanced instruments. The probe was originally named Solar Probe Plus, but it was renamed Parker right before the scientist's 90th birthday in 2017. This is the first time a spacecraft has been named after a living person. Parker died in 2022, but he lived to see his namesake launched.

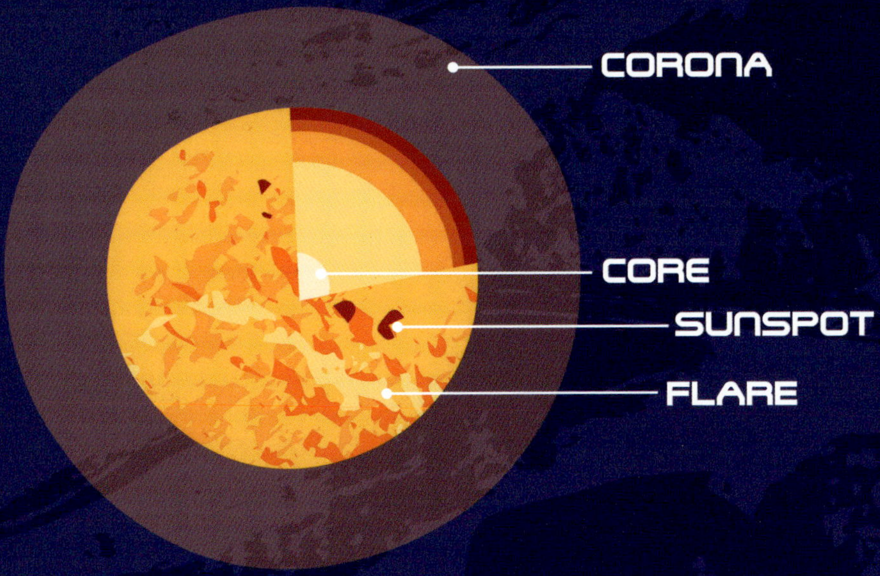

This picture shows different parts of the sun.

Another of Parker's tools is called the Electromagnetic Fields Investigation (FIELDS). This measures the electric and magnetic fields and waves around the sun. Scientists know that the sun's magnetism is an important part of the solar wind, and with this instrument, they hope to learn more about why that is.

Finally, Parker holds two instruments that together are called the Integrated Science Investigation of the Sun (IS☉IS). IS☉IS will use a **mass spectrometer** to weigh and sort particles that move past the probe. It has two instruments so it can cover a wider energy range. The more particles IS☉IS can measure, the more information scientists will have to work with.

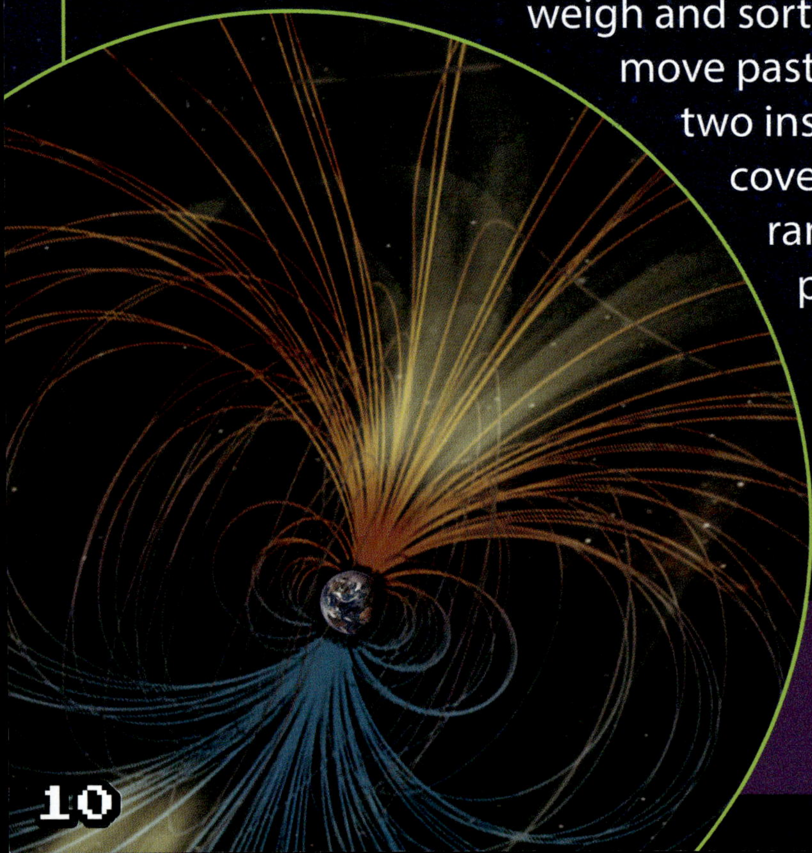

EARTH'S MAGNETIC FIELD

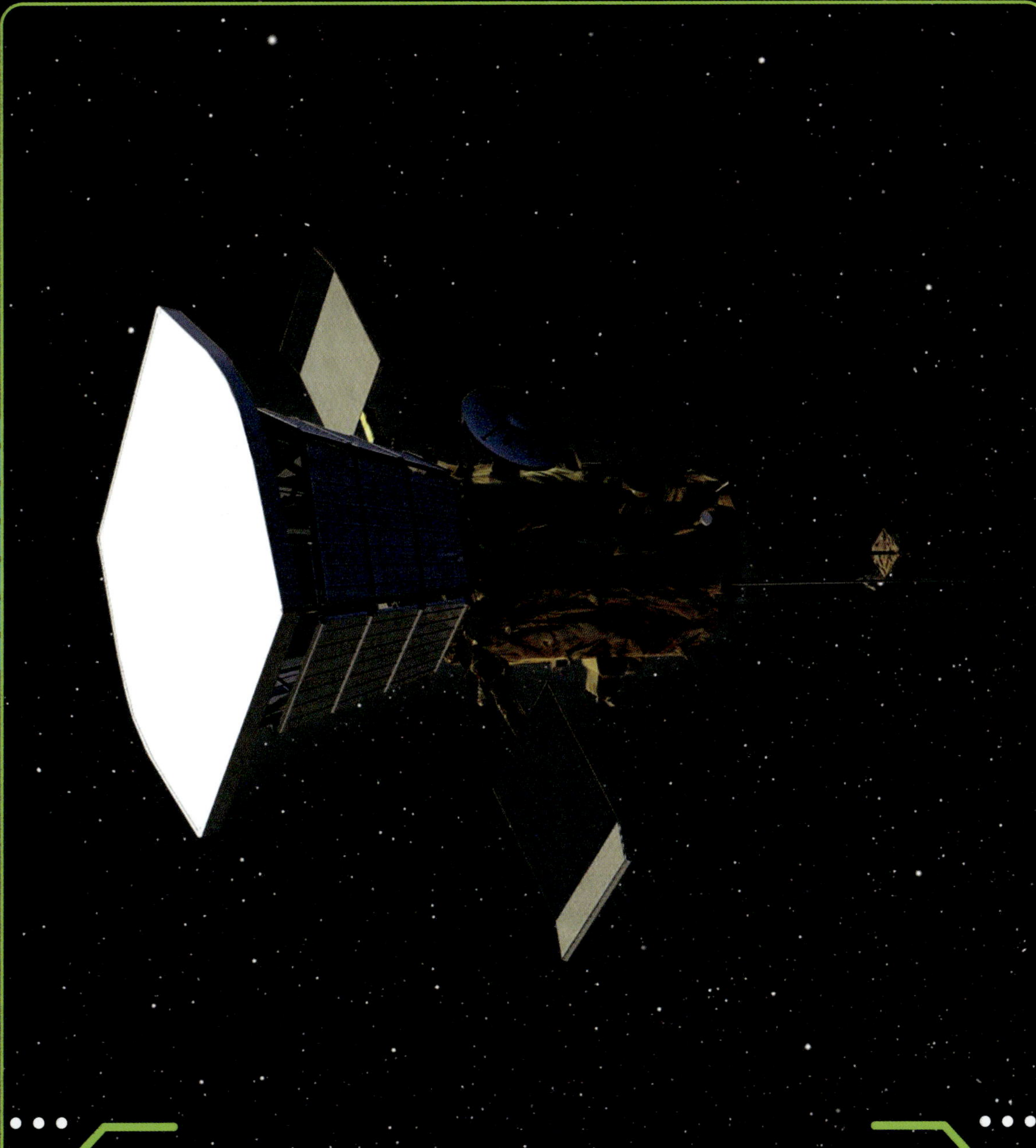

The Parker Solar Probe's instruments will give scientists a lot of new information about the sun.

TRAVEL PATH

Parker's trajectory, or travel path, is not direct. Instead of flying directly at the sun, the probe is designed to make 24 passes, getting a little closer each time. This will help scientists compare various measurements to see how they change closer to the sun.

To help it complete these passes, the probe will fly past Venus seven times. This will give it a boost from Venus's gravity. The gravity assist, as scientists call it, will give the probe a fast push in the direction of the sun. If Parker did not fly past Venus, it would slow down over time and finally come to a complete stop, drifting aimlessly in space. It might end up going in entirely the wrong direction.

VENUS

FALLING WITH STYLE

On Earth, gravity always pulls people and things down toward the planet's center. In space, an object's gravity pulls smaller objects toward it. However, unlike on Earth, the smaller object's trajectory can keep it from falling into the more massive object. In addition to stopping the probe from slowing down before it reaches the sun, the gravity assist from Venus helps it keep a trajectory that will stop it from falling into the sun.

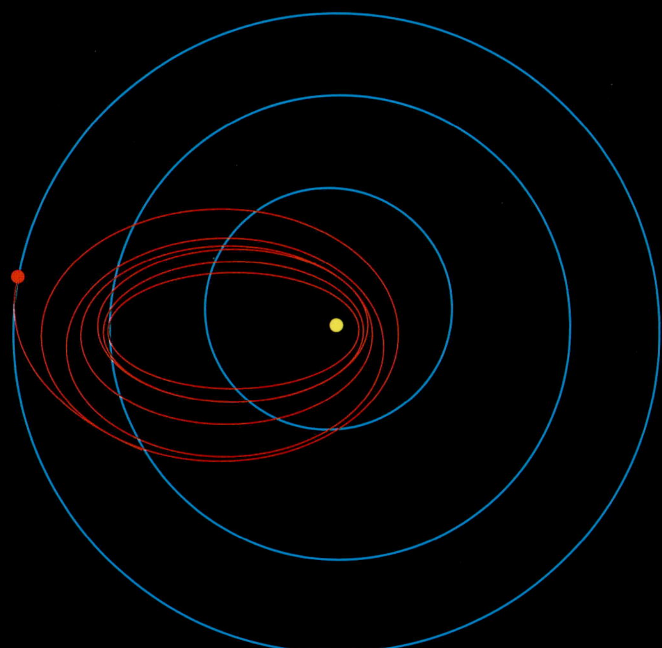

This picture shows the roundabout trajectory Parker (red dot) has taken to get close to the sun (yellow dot). The blue circles represent the orbits of Mercury, Venus, and Earth.

BREAKING RECORDS

One of the most amazing things about the Parker Solar Probe is how fast it can go. In July 2024, it traveled at more than 500 times the speed of sound! Scientists say it will move even faster when it makes its next pass, even closer to the sun. This makes the probe the fastest-moving object ever made by humans.

The reason for its incredible speed is the size of the sun. The larger an object is, the more gravity it **exerts** on objects nearby. The sun is the largest object in our solar system. When the probe gets close to it, gravity pulls it in. The closer the probe is to the sun, the stronger the pull gravity exerts on it. This makes the probe fly faster as it gets closer.

NASA KNOWLEDGE

In many common conditions, sound travels at a speed of about 761 miles (1,225 km) per hour. If a person could travel at Parker's top speed of 430,000 miles (692,000 km) per hour, they could travel from San Francisco to Washington, D.C., in 20 seconds.

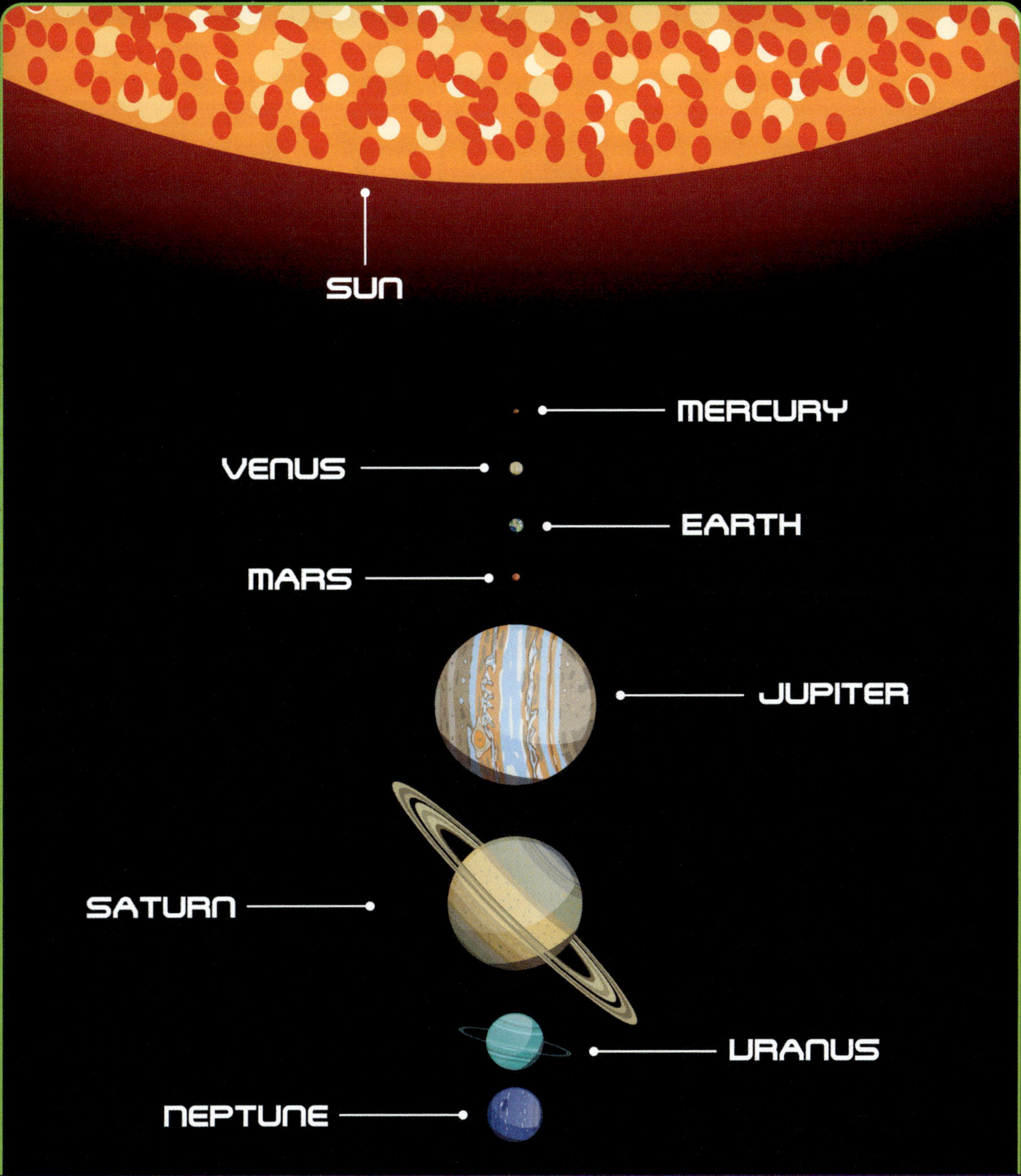

The sun contains 99 percent of all the matter in the solar system.

WITHSTANDING THE HEAT

The probe's speed is one of the things that helps it survive its close encounters with the sun. It flies past so quickly that it is only briefly exposed to the more intense levels of heat and radiation. Of course, the heat and radiation are still an issue in space, even some distance from the sun. To make sure Parker would stay in working order long enough to complete its mission, NASA engineers had to address those issues when they designed the probe.

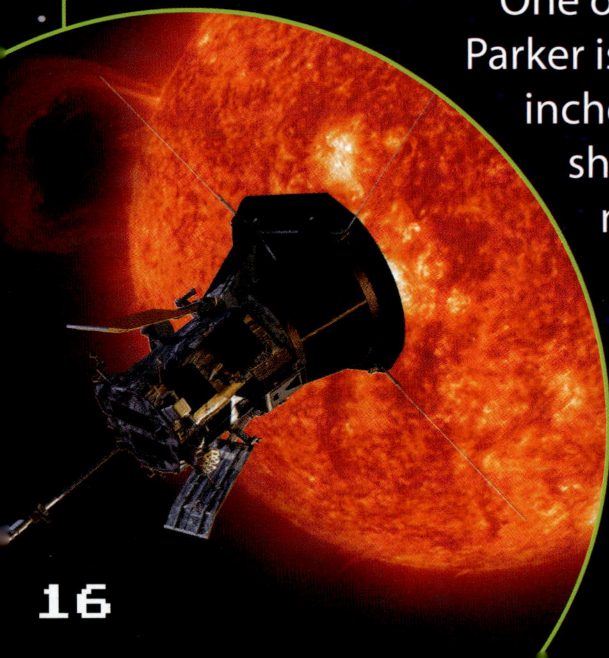

One of the features that protects Parker is a heat shield that is 4.5 inches (11.43 cm) thick. The shield's thickness and the material it's made of help it withstand temperatures up to 2,500 degrees F (1,377 degrees C). Behind the shield, Parker's instruments never reach more than 85 degrees F (29 degrees C).

USING NATURE

Parker has solar panels on it so it can use the sun's energy as a power source. The solar panels move, so they can cover themselves to prevent the probe from getting too much heat and power at once. The panels also have a gallon of water pumping through them. The water absorbs the heat and flows into the probe's **radiator**. The radiator releases the heat into space, the water cools, and then it is pumped through the solar panels again to repeat the process.

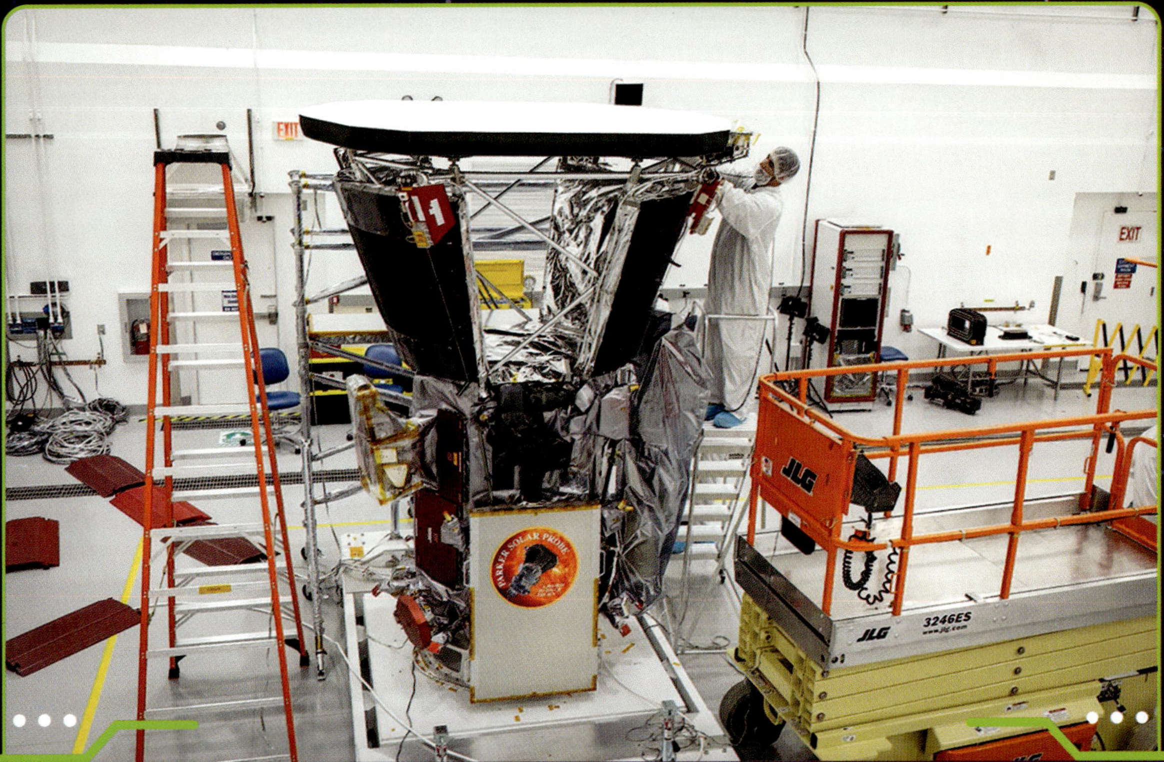

This picture shows NASA engineers attaching the heat shield to the probe.

Another thing that helps Parker survive close to the sun is that the corona is very thin. This means the particles are spread out, so the probe is exposed to fewer of them at one time. This is the difference between temperature and heat. Temperature is a measure of how fast particles are moving. Heat is a measure of how much energy they transfer to an object.

The sun's corona has a high temperature. Its particles move very fast. However, because they are spread out across a large area, Parker doesn't run into many of them. If the particles don't touch the spacecraft, they can't transfer their energy to it in the form of heat.

NASA KNOWLEDGE

When a gas is superheated, it becomes a state of matter called plasma. The sun is made up of gases, and these become plasma in the corona. This happens when the atoms in a gas split into smaller parts and move around freely.

When a pot of water is placed on a stove, the energy from the stove burner transfers heat to the pot. This makes the temperature of the water rise.

SAMPLING THE CORONA

On April 28, 2021, the Parker Space Probe became the first spacecraft to touch the sun when it flew close enough to **sample** the corona. The information it sent back to Earth has already helped scientists get closer to answering questions about the corona, such as what is heating it and how it gets so hot so fast.

When Parker first got close to the sun, it found hundreds of s-shaped bends in the solar wind. Scientists named these bends "switchbacks" because they temporarily reverse the magnetic field. Some scientists believed the energy stored in the switchbacks was the answer to the coronal heating mystery. If the switchbacks formed in the center of the sun and moved outward into the corona, it would explain where the heat was coming from.

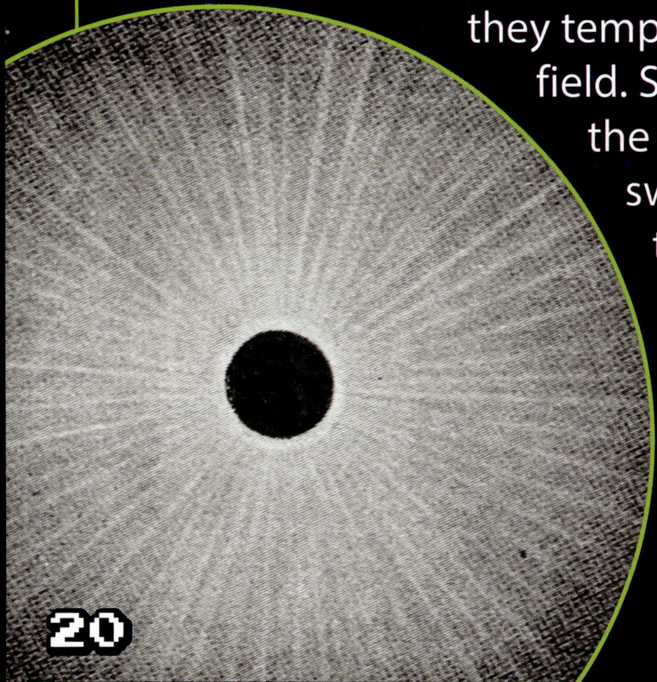

The sun's switchbacks were named after the s-shaped sections of a road that temporarily reverse the direction of the road.

RULED OUT

After studying the switchbacks further, scientists have ruled them out as a possible solution to the coronal heating mystery. This is because switchbacks are not present in the corona. Scientists are not fully sure yet what causes the switchbacks to form. However, they do believe they know where they come from: magnetic collisions, or crashes, on the sun's surface.

Even though NASA has ruled out switchbacks as a cause for coronal heating, they have not yet ruled them out as a source of the solar wind. Scientists already know that the solar wind's speed is affected by the magnetic field. They hope that studying switchbacks will help them figure out exactly which part of the sun the solar wind comes from.

A NEW THEORY

Although the switchbacks are not the direct source of the corona's heat, some scientists think they could still play a role. For instance, the energy from the magnetic collisions might heat up the corona before forming switchbacks in the solar wind. Scientists will have to study the switchbacks much more before they can say if this is what's happening.

This picture shows how some of the particles swirl around the corona and dip back toward the surface of the sun, while others fly away from the sun.

THE SOLAR WIND BOUNDARY

Parker also used its WISPR tool to image the solar wind boundary. This is the point at which the corona becomes the solar wind. It is officially known as the Alfvén surface. The pictures show objects called coronal streamers. These are giant columns of solar particles that make the Alfvén surface **textured** rather than smooth. The pictures would be impossible to take from Earth. Parker was able to take them because of the angle at which it flew through the corona.

Scientists plan to use WISPR's pictures and other measurements from Parker to match the coronal streamers with areas of activity on the sun's surface. This will help them track the movement of solar particles from their origin, or starting point, all the way out through the solar wind.

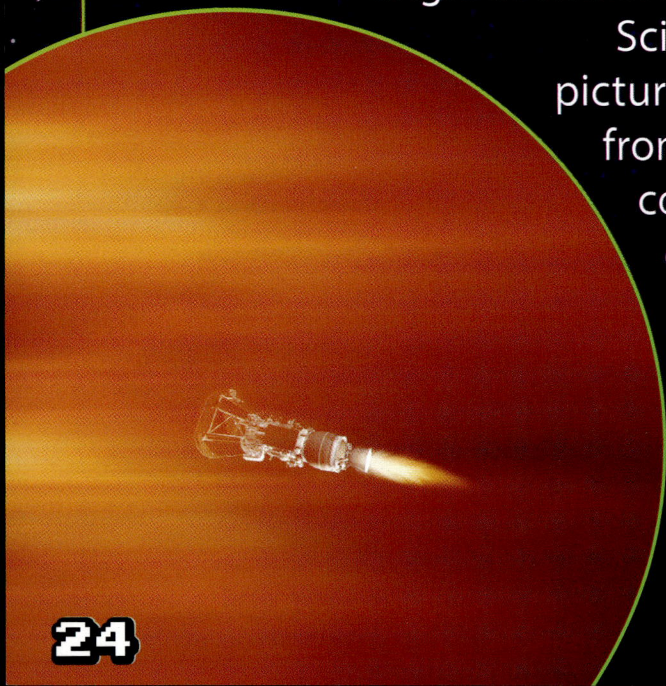

NASA KNOWLEDGE

In the corona, the particles swirl around and dip back toward the surface of the sun. Once the particles pass the Alfvén surface, they do not move back toward the surface. Instead, they flow outward into space, becoming the solar wind.

The Alfvén surface is named after Hannes Alfvén, a Swedish scientist who made many discoveries about the sun's magnetic field and the ways it interacts with Earth's atmosphere.

USING INFORMATION

Scientists have already started studying the information Parker is sending back to Earth, and they will continue to do so in the future. One of the ways they plan to use the information is to make better **predictions** about space weather that can help keep people and equipment safe, including when a solar storm will hit and which parts of space will receive the most radiation.

For example, during solar storms, satellites are more likely to be damaged by the sun's radiation. If satellite operators knew about a solar storm in advance, they might be able to shut down parts of the satellite to stop those parts from being damaged. They might also be able to move the satellite to a position where it will receive less radiation.

SATELLITE NETWORK

NASA KNOWLEDGE

Space weather affects many things, including the health and safety of astronauts and how well satellites, power lines, and cell phone towers work.

Satellites help predict the weather on Earth, connect us to the internet, and do much more. When they don't work, there are often problems on the ground.

PARKER'S FUTURE

Parker is expected to complete its 24th and final pass of the sun by the end of 2025. After that, the probe will continue making passes as long as it is able to do so. Once the probe stops working, the pressure of the sun's heat on its heat shield will make it start to rotate, or spin. Because only part of the probe is designed to withstand the sun's heat, this rotation will allow the sun to damage the other parts of the probe. Soon, the damage will become too severe, and Parker will break apart. Its pieces will settle into a regular orbit around the sun. Until that happens, scientists will learn all they can from Parker's measurements.

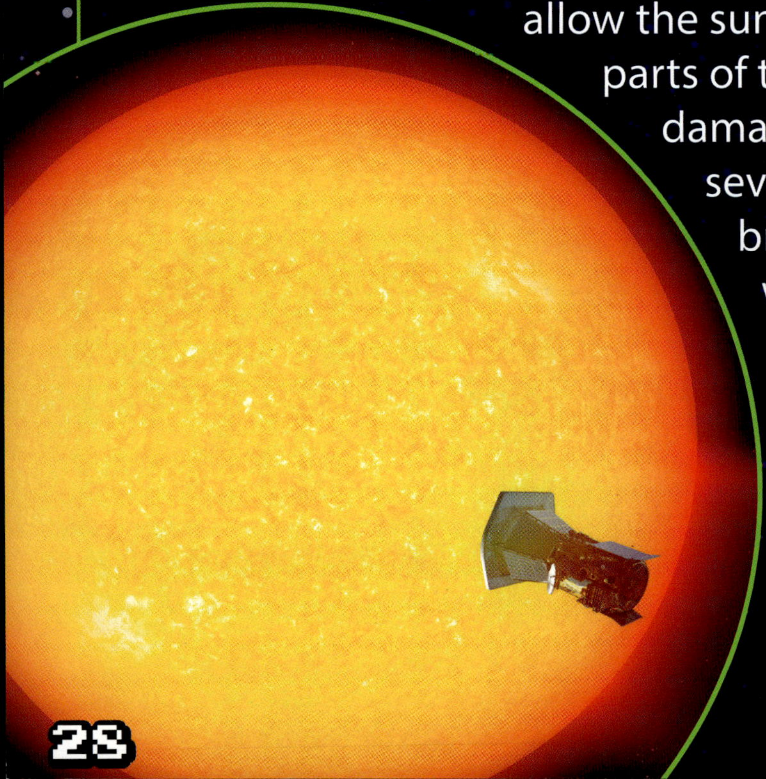

Even the hottest day on Earth is thousands of degrees cooler than the corona. Once Parker's shield stops protecting it, there is no way the probe will survive the intense heat and radiation.

GLOSSARY

cancer: A sometimes deadly sickness in which cells grow in a way they should not, often forming tumors, or growths, that harm the body.

corona: The outermost part of the atmosphere of a star.

exert: To put forth effort.

heliosphere: The region of space that is affected by the sun or solar wind.

mass spectrometer: An instrument that measures the mass-to-charge ratio of charged particles.

prediction: A guess about what will happen in the future.

radiation: Waves of energy.

radiator: A tool that transfers heat from a fluid inside to an area or object outside.

sample: To take a part of something; a part that represents the whole.

specialized: Pertaining to one particular job, skill, or purpose.

textured: Having a rough or uneven surface.

FOR MORE INFORMATION

BOOKS

Bard, Jonathan, and Mariel Bard. *Great Ball of Fire: Studying the Sun.* New York, NY: Gareth Stevens Publishing, 2021.

Rhatigan, Joe, and Beth Adelman. *Parker Solar Probe: Touching the Sun.* Minneapolis, MN: Lerner Publications, 2024.

Stratton, Connor. *Space Exploration.* Lake Elmo, MN: Focus Readers, 2023.

WEBSITES

Kiddle: Parker Solar Probe Facts for Kids
kids.kiddle.co/Parker_Solar_Probe
Take a look at Parker's mission timeline as well as some amazing pictures.

NASA: All About the Sun
spaceplace.nasa.gov/all-about-the-sun
Find out what scientists already know about our closest star.

NASA: ParkerBot
parkersolarprobe.jhuapl.edu/parkerbot
Ask ParkerBot questions about the Parker Solar Probe.

INDEX